C000000349

The Pennings of the Poisonous Pixie's Book of Poetry

RACHEL RHODES-PUCKETT

A lyrical collection of musings, thoughts, experiences and
perceptions by Rachel Rhodes-Puckett.

ISBN: 1974581101
ISBN 13: 9781974581108

Dedication

This book is dedicated to my parents, Pamela and John Puckett –
love you to the moon and back and beyond!

Table of Contents

The Poisonous Pixie

I am the Poisonous Pixie
I wield my poisoned pen
I rant and rave and contemplate
And dish the dirt on (some) men

It brings me so much joy
To vent and find expression
In rhyming words and symbolism
As I learn my daily lessons

And if we should come into contact
And you should make an impression
You too could find yourself immortalised
In a lyrical form of expression

So please be nice –
For if you're naughty you'll know
You'll end up in a poem
And on my blog you'll go

And then up on to Facebook
For all the world to see
So like I said, be nice
Or you'll be a victim of the Poisonous Pixie!

Motivation

My palate of colours
Is rich and derives
From life's encounters,
And emotions which arise

When the impulse strikes
I dip in the brush
And paint with words
Impassioned, in a rush

A lyrical snapshot
Of something that impacted
My sensibilities
And how I reacted

In this I've found
My passion it seems
My raison d'être
A blessed release

And the rule of thumb
I'm told in this life
Is do what makes you happy
And it does so I write

The work itself
May not always be pretty
In the eye of the beholder
Is beauty – not a pity

One person's junk
Is another's treasure
Still relevant
In equal measure

Mentally ill
Or an artist of sorts
I need an outlet
For my thoughts

Creative types
Are misunderstood
They're often tortured
And sometimes judged

But the fruits of their labour
Permeate our culture
Without it life would be barren
It is essential, like agriculture

That I write from personal experience
Is an act of my own volition
Every expression of 'art' in existence
Stems in part from the human condition

If you happen to know
Whence my inspiration came
I must consider you a friend
Thus from condemnation please refrain

The work I produce could be fact
It could indeed be fiction
But produce the work I must
It's something of an affliction

It's no mean feat for me
To publish a creation
Any kindred spirit will know
The mantle I've undertaken

It's terrifying to exhibit
In the public domain
To perform in front of an audience
And expose yourself that way

But it seems I am a poet
Maybe an aspiring bard
And I realise that I love it
To understand that you may find hard

If it's not for you
Then that's ok
But some of us
We're born this way.

Just Sayin

Every situation
Has the potential to be a gift
Sometimes it's apparent
Sometimes hidden in the mist

Every encounter you have
With another living being
Feeds your soul somehow
And it evolves, your spirit freeing

Actions, words, experience
Are opportunities for magnificence
And magnificently when your essence reacts
There's a golden chance to learn from that

For all of us are students
Upon this earthly plane
And until we graduate
We'll encounter pleasure and sometimes pain

A plethora of emotions
We sentient people feel
Sometimes they shake us to the core
We're knocked off course, we reel

When that happens I crave expression
Or I know I'll fall apart
I'm compelled to put it into verse
Some might call it art

It's all subjective anyway
And I'm not saying this compulsion is right
But one thing's for sure, hand on heart
Writing actually saved my life.

Clarity

The veil has lifted
I see the truth
The stark reality
My misspent youth

No space for blame
Just circumstance
We all deserve
A second chance

A time to live
A time to die
And yes you may
Want to ask why

A time for answers
A time for change
One thing's for sure
It can't stay the same

We say goodbye
Let go with love
Restore our faith
In what's above

We then move on
Into the light
And try our best
To do what's right

We're only human
And in the end
We make mistakes
Let's not pretend.

Note To Self

Little girl
Protect your dreams
For they are precious
Such precious things

Keep them safe
Inside your heart
And place the key
Inside a star

The angels have
A job to do
Watch over them
And over you

And when it's safe
To take them out
They will come true
I have no doubt.

The time is nigh
And you are ready
Just keep your nerve
And take it steady

Sing it loud
And play it clear
So all the world
Cannot but hear

And then rejoice
In what's to come
Take a bow
The job is done.

The Twilight Zone

Raging voices
Inside her head
Possessive spirits
In her ear ranted

"The world is ending
Doomsday has come!"
The sky turned red
Nowhere to run

Hands over her eyes
None free to steer
Foetal inside the car
Doomsday indeed was here!

A knock to the left
A bang to the right
Spinning in circles
A blinding flash of white light

Then nothingness came
Out of her body was she
Floating in a tunnel
For what seemed an eternity

Then Raphael spoke
And to her senses she came
A man walked towards her
As it started to rain

Pierced by icy chills
To the essence of her being
Trembling and convulsing
Penetrating shock set in

Out of nowhere an ambulance
Then did appear
He'd radioed for help
And now it was here

"Take your arms off, take your legs off,
Climb out of your body"
Not believing what she was hearing
The paramedic encouraged

Her to do just that
She obeyed, as was right
For nobody was laughing
On this surreal night

Guided to the ambulance
They lay her down
Covered her in a blanket
Arms crossed, safe and sound

She finally closed her eyes
As they began to move
But it felt like taking off
They weren't driving, they flew!

Sucked into a vortex
Through dimensions of time
Twisting and a-turning
Rapid rollercoaster ride

Then she heard weeping
Raised her eyelids to see
A blonde pretty lady
Crying tears of grief

She asked "Are you ok?"
"Am I ok? You're dead!"
Startled she passed out
Disturbed by what was said

She awakened as the pawn
In some supernatural game
In the emergency ward
As 'good' and 'evil' a battle waged

Over ownership of her soul
So petrified was she
Unconsciousness set in
Oblivian, sleep

She awoke to find her father
Sitting by her side
He'd come, he had found her!
Relieved she cried

Now could she go home?
The doctors said "No"
She'd really had enough
And she wanted that so

She ran for the door
But restrained was she
They held her down
She couldn't break free

She wrestled and writhed
Arms bound behind her back
Then she got away
And gave someone a slap

It was self defence, retaliation
She thought she was attacked
But the police then descended
And, cuffed, that was that

Bundled into a cage
Inside a van
Driven away
Thrown in the can

Manhandled, mistreated
Battered and bruised
She began to sing
To keep herself amused

Like a canary
All through the night
Her entire back catalogue
Did she recite

Until the door swung open
And people came inside
One by one in procession
Something of a tribe

"Come with us" they said
"We'll make you a star
We're filming a documentary
About crashes in cars"

But the voices returned
And forced her to stay
Telling her that
The devil was at play

In no uncertain terms
She ordered them to leave
Then slumbered on the cold, hard floor
In her prison weeds

Next morning she was transported
To a fate worse than death
With every turn of events
She plunged deeper into the mess

Incarcerated in an asylum
Naked, stripped of her dignity
Intoxicated, medicated
No grip on reality

Dangerous and squalid
Like a living hell on earth
No waking from this nightmare
Defecation everywhere

How had it come to this?
Had her karma hit all at once?
Like The Falling Tower
She was struck by a thunderbolt

Broken apart and abused
Subjected to torture so horrid
To the authorities did she submit
This was worse than doing porridge

For many weeks did she remain
In that place absent of peace
Until one blessed day it came to pass
That she was at last released

Scarred was she for life
Shaken to the core
Had she dreamt it all?
She knew not anymore

Tattooed on her mind
Is that to which she was exposed
So paranormal it could be a movie
Doing time in the twilight zone.

Diamond In The Rough

Been crawling through the gutter
Caked in mud
Looking for that diamond
In the rough
Staring at the stars
Couldn't climb the ladder
Kept on sliding down
Had to try harder

Helping hands at times
Slapped me in the face
A dog eat dog world
A dangerous rat race
But I'm still in the running
And I'm not giving up
I'm a tough mother
With a fire in my gut

Do you believe in God?
In a higher power?
The jury is all out
But in my darkest hour

I saw a blinding light
And came out of my body
I walked out of the wreckage
Without a scratch on me

I was on a ride
Was it heaven? Was it hell?
Was it just my mind?
Failing me as well?
When nothing seems real
And you want to know the truth
Who do you believe?
Who can give you proof?

Humans can be flawed
The system is all fucked
Saviours come and go
But some run out of luck
The truth is often silenced
Through fear of retribution
Can't stomach all these lies
It affects my constitution

Who wrote it anyway?
Why should it adapt?
Maybe I feel sick
Cause I was fed such crap

Maybe if the sustenance
Was pure and came from love
The toxins in my system
Couldn't me corrupt

My filter would be clear
My body would be nourished
My mind would stand a chance
My troubled soul would flourish
Then maybe I could live
A life of pure bliss
And peace would be on earth
Instead of a fantasy in the abyss.

Apocalyptic Episode

Been struck by lightning
Blown apart
Exposed myself
In the form of art

Like the falling tower
I couldn't make it stop
I didn't see it coming
It's like a bomb has dropped

I'm sitting in the rubble
Examining the ruins
I'm wondering if the fallout
Could be my undoing

But something deep inside
Is telling me to wait
Something is unfolding
To do with my own fate

The explosion was the key
To breaking free of chains
The death of my old self
The recycling of the remains

The birth of something new
The dawn of a new era
A time to speak the truth
And live without fear

A time to atone
Forgive and then to let go
A time to heal myself
And maybe feel sorrow

But also a time to rejoice
In all that is good
And a time to be thankful
For those that showed me love.

Angst

A sudden flush of terror
Heart beats ten to the dozen
Palpitations and cold sweats
Rigid, almost wooden

Suddenly it's panic stations
The power to think is lost
You feel the need to flee
Run away, but at what cost?

Stressed and scared, your stomach flips
Brain races, you feel sick
Where did it all go wrong, you cry?
How did you miss a trick?

The anxious mind is purgatory
And what's more there's no escape
Cloaked in horror it weighs you down
You wear it like a cape

You need to chill
To calm your head
Be anywhere but here

But how to escape
Your own sick thoughts
When crippled all over by fear?

Hit the bottle?
Have a fag?
Do anything to block it out

You have to keep
A lid on it
But really you want to shout

"Help me, I can't stand it!
Ease the pain I'm in,
Comfort me, I'm at breaking point
This battle I can't win!"

Then all of a sudden
The wave has passed
You snap out of it
Just like that!

A gibbering wreck
You take a breath
And think:
'I am such a t**t!'

You brush it off
Shake yourself down
Tell yourself that you're fine

But deep down you know
It'll come back someday
And catch you by surprise

Anxiety, anxiety
Be gone, leave me in peace
You're twisting my sobriety
I want to be released

One day I will conquer you
Without the need for drugs
Holistically I'll vanquish you
No trace you'll leave, no smudge.

The Volcano

Keep your distance
Whilst I erupt
This molten lava
Is coming up
The urge to purge
Is blowing me open
Get out of the way
Whilst I'm being outspoken

I can't protect you
From what's to come
But equally I can no longer keep mum
This pyroclastic surge
May cause some destruction
But the chamber is bursting
The magma craves expression

It's been bubbling inside
And now it's overflowing
Who will feel it's force
I have no way of knowing
But it's a natural reaction
To what I'm going through
I'm overwhelmed with emotion
And this isn't about you.

Aspiring To Wholeness

Bi Polarity
Two extremes
Opposite ends
That strive to meet
In the middle
Where all is balanced
Equilibrium
Can be such a challenge
Two halves of a whole
That need to unite
In order to function
Without a fight

Gemini
The sign of the twins
A blessing and a curse
Or so it seems
Divided again
Or two halves of a whole?
Separate
Or of the same soul?

Brother and sister
From the same source
Family yet
Estranged and divorced

Two sides of a coin
Conjoined in the middle
By bronze, silver and gold
Such precious metals
The struggle to marry
The yin and yang
To complete the puzzle
And be at one
Something out of kilter
So many conflicting parts
But the fragments are coming together
I can feel it in my heart.

Reach Out

When your mental health
Comes under attack
And you're feeling like
You're going to crack

When there's nowhere to run
For you can't escape yourself
What should you do?
How should you get help?

Should you block it all out?
Anaesthetise the pain?
Self-medicate, self-harm
Self-destruct, go insane?

Sink into a hole?
Close the door on the world?
Suffer in silence?
Let it take a hold?

I really don't think so
Try to find a better way
Talk it out with someone
Maybe meditate or pray

Put a pen to paper
Allow it to come through
Don't keep it bottled up inside
If it could mean the end of you

Please don't ignore it
It won't just go away
Reach out, find a cure
So you can live another day

It's time to erase the stigma
Surrounding the disturbed mind
Anyone can have a meltdown
At any point in time

Could be me, could be you,
Could be her next door
And it's purgatory when it's strikes
And you're writhing on the floor

Self respect down the drain
You struggle and toil to stand tall
The last thing such victims need
Is judgement, condemnation and scorn

It's just a little blip
It requires understanding
Compassion, love and patience
And utmost care when handling

If we can eradicate the fear and judgment
Sufferers will be able to shout
Not ashamedly imprison themselves
And perhaps seek the ultimate way out

It's an illness like any other
And can be treated in a myriad of ways
So please, FFS, reach out!
Get help for goodness sake.

Lessons In Love

You can't choose who you love
You can't make them love you back
You can't choose how they treat you
The only choice is how you react

If you're love is unrequited
Or even ill received
If it's too much for them to take
If it's ill perceived

Don't love them less
Just walk away
Find another outlet
Because if it hurts its not ok
And something's wrong about it

Love is unconditional
It can't be bought and sold
And if you choose to express it
You have to let it go.

The Key To Free

If you've suffered abuse
Don't face it alone
Seek the strength to speak out
And get help soon

Don't think it's your fault
The issue is theirs
Know that it's wrong
They are not taking care

Whatever it's nature
If it hurts it's not right
If it makes you feel bad
If you have to fight

To protect yourself
Or, worse, stay silent
Find a way to escape
Live free of violence

The abuser is sick
And not of sound mind
If they disrespect you
They are deeply unkind

Love yourself more
Than you love them
Turn and walk away
Because things won't change

They need help
And you to do
Just forget about them
And focus on you.

Harnessing Anger

Yesterday I was angry
The rage burned deep within
White hot searing heat
Permeating every limb

The flames did lick my tightened chest
Threatening to consume
Suppressing it was difficult
Not something I could do

So I harnessed it through writing
And constructed a cage of words
A little spark did still escape
But I feel it was deserved

And now the anger has passed
Damage limitation was a success
Emotions are natural thus hard to control
We can regulate them at best.

Cursed

Time to let go
But finding it hard
Strings are tugging
At my heart

When you've been tied to someone
For so long
And you need to walk away
You have to be strong

Seems an impossible task
Willpower non-existent
Head telling you the right thing to do
Emotions pulling you in the opposite direction

How do you switch it off?
When someone is under your skin?
Cursing through your veins?
Not physically here but within?

It only took a moment
To undo all that hard work
Progress that had been made
Discarded, cast away, shirked

Now to begin again
Building up that wall
Encasing those feelings in an iron coffin
Burying it deep beneath, in a vault

Forgetting all over again
How it was when it was great
Trying to only focus
On the bad times and the hate

But how can you focus on the hate?
When all there really is is love?
When seeing them again takes your breath away?
When you're insanely thinking you can never have enough?

Cursed I am it seems
Afflicted by that which has no cure
I just wish he'd spared me this
Never returned to these helpless shores

Who knows how long I will toil
And writhe in this agony
Until blessed numbness sets in
And once again I am free.

Rejection

Rejection is subjective
Though it hurts and that's the truth
How you deal with it depends
On how you feel about you

If you love yourself more
The sooner you'll bounce back
If you lack self worth
Try to work on that

Build yourself up
So that if you are affected
The wound won't cut so deep
Should you ever be rejected

Know it happens to us all
At one time or another
So softly, softly go
With your sisters and your brothers

One day it could be you
Doing the rejecting
So be as kind as you can
For the recipient deserves protecting

They are human too
We're all in the same boat
A little consideration for each other
Will keep us all afloat.

Goodbye

I'm so full of emotion
It's so hard to say goodbye
But I am moving into the distance
I got no more tears to cry

I've heard you said it's over baby
To the world but not to me
You disappeared without a trace not maybe
Nothing left, not a thing to see

And it hurts
But I'm done with the pain
And I will never be the same
Again, again

Yes it hurts
But it is for the best
Time to go and leave the past to rest
My friend, my friend

So goodbye…
I hope the future's kind to you
Goodbye, goodbye
So goodbye…

Good luck where you are going to
Goodbye, goodbye

There is a space where you once were
I'll admit that much is true

But something better's coming my way
And it's nothing to do with you

You say that I meant nothing to you
Well it's funny how people change
When it was me you called in your darkest hour
And me you needed again

And it hurts
But I'm done with the pain
And I will never be the same
Again, again

Yes it hurts
But it is for the best
Time to go and leave the past to rest
My friend, my friend

So goodbye
I hope the future's kind to you
Goodbye, goodbye
So goodbye
Good luck where you are going to
Goodbye, goodbye.

The River Of Life

The river of life keeps a-flowing
The dickheads of life, coming and going
We victims have no way of knowing
Why these dweebs gravitate towards us as they're sowing

We attract them like magnets, like moths to a flame
They love us, then piss off, leaving us wondering whose
to blame
And we, wounded souls, will never be the same
Whilst they jump on to the next and start sowing again

I wish the river of life would drown the little shits
Who've broken our hearts and left us in bits
As they move on, get married, sprout kids
We pick up the pieces, have therapy, get pissed

I'll never understand why these bastards get on
Whilst their broken exes limp, searching in vain for the one
Why they morph into respectable, family-minded gents
Whilst their exes get bitter and moan and resent

We have to believe they weren't meant for us
They treated us like dirt, made us cry, made us cuss
And we were too nice to be shackled to such toads
Our princes will come, they're just lost in the post!

Battle Of The Sexes

Double standards
Unspoken rules
Too quick to judge
The bloody fools

Perilous waters
Not for the faint-hearted
Keep your wits about you
You might be outsmarted

Fuelled by alcohol
The social norm
Though it blurs your judgement
And loosens your tongue

Suddenly your guard
Has massively been let down
You find yourself surrendering
Animal instinct wears the crown

So you succumb
To the pleasures of the flesh
It's what you need right now
Nothing more and nothing less

But when the dust settles
The inevitable verdict will be passed
The female of the species
Should have kept her legs crossed

It's a man's world after all
They call all the shots
And them's the rules, you stupid girl
Thus this battle you have lost

Enjoy yourself?
How very dare you!
You spoiled the game
Now he can't bear you

A modern woman
Who pleases herself
Can't be trusted
Especially if she has wealth

It rattles them, you see
If she can survive alone
Ignites their insecurity
Their masculinity suffers a blow

So off they scurry
In search of shelter
And the fairytale princess
Who yearns for her saviour

These Amazonian 'abominations'
For such as he are all too much
His ego cannot withstand the force
Of a woman full of lust

Worldly and strong
Independent and wise
Intimidating to the mice of men
Something of a nasty surprise

Well, it sure as hell aint my problem
If you can't handle this
Off you go, you little frog
You clearly won't transform with a kiss.

Smited

Ouch it hurts
A lash of the whip
I recoil at the smite
I sting, I was bit

I retreat in shock
Not what I expected
I expected nothing
I wasn't protected

The breath knocked out of me
So swift came the blow
Should've trusted my instincts
Should've left well alone

Nausea sets in
Tummy upset
Good intentions
Unwelcomed, ill met

Now a dead end
A full stop, a brick wall
Nowhere to go
I shrink, feel small

Shrivelled and foetal
I take refuge in bed
Now for a lobotomy
To erase it from my head

The ripple effect
My whole being atremble
Tears start to well
I suppress them but they assemble

How to process this shit
Right now I don't know
I feel like taking action
But should leave well alone

Is retaliation
The wisest move?
I'm wounded and frail
My strength subdued

Deadlocked it seems
In chains, boxed in
Immobilised, indecisive
Intuition dim

Better sit this one out
Meditate upon it
Reflect and learn
Though I'm stunned, astonished

Defeated I suppose
Come down from a high
I crash back to earth
Wings clipped, can't fly.

E-No!-Ji

Death by emoji
The conversation killer
Defeated by words
Not a bean spiller

Elusive and vague
Open to interpretation
Depends on the context
Yet causes frustration

In dating terms
When the stakes are high
Text 'etiquette'
Drives you bloody wild

The kissometer factor
Is an example of that
Do you count them or not
Send the same amount back?

What if the levels are variable
What the 'F' does that mean?
Initially you get none
Then you wind up with THREE!

I'm damned if I know the answer
How to play this stupid game
So complicated and technical
Enough to turn you insane

Somebody give me a manual
Decode the information
Or rather just use ENGLISH
And WORDS for clarification!

Spiderman

So we stepped into the mire
Came at it from different angles
We forgot we were playing with fire
Intoxicated, we threw off the shackles

We gave into desire
In that moment it felt right
The chemistry was palpable
Although we put up a fight

I didn't know your story
Hadn't told you mine
Complexitites stayed under wraps
We got on with having a good time

Flickers of signs were there
If only we had listened
And read them right, taken our time
A future could have glistened

But in the light of day
It ultimately transpires
That we're both in different places
At opposite ends of the shires

Wreckless, yes, but criminals, no
I guess our luck was in
Two decent people who lost their way
Temporarily throwing caution to the wind

Regret is futile, we're fallible, human
And wisdom comes through learning
From our mistakes and from forgiveness
Even when passion is burning

The dating scene is a labyrinth of landmines
It's sometimes necessary to traverse
Relationships at any time
Bring out the best and also the worst

In both the sexes – so many rules,
Agendas and social conditioning
Factors that conflict sometimes
And sensibilities that need protecting

But ultimately we all want the same thing
To be loved and to give love
To share our lives with another being
Who's got our backs and doesn't judge

It's trepidatious this life we lead
– I don't want to go it alone
So I lent myself to you that night
Thinking maybe you could be someone

I could walk this path with
For a little while
Make some music with
Relearn how to smile

Have a little dance with
Act out an awesome scene
Maybe it was premature
And common sense should have intervened

But my intentions here were pure
And in that moment I picked someone
Under different circumstances I could adore
A gentleman and good fun

You tell me you're not ready
And indeed I respect that
So I'm letting you go, right here, right now
Reluctantly, yes, but intact..

Aftermath

The aftermath
A barren plane
Nothingness
Is what remains

Easy come
Easy go
The dust that settles
Like melting snow

No foundation
On which to rest
Nothing of substance
Just emptiness

A drop in the ocean
Diluted, dissipated
A mere collision
On a course segregated

The emotional impact
The only trace
Of an interlude
That once took place

A shooting star
In the vast moonlit sky
Too hot it combusted
Vaporised and died

Burnt itself out
In spectacular fashion
Up in smoke
Almost like it never happened

Perhaps it was but a dream
A phantom bump in the night
That like a vampire was vanquished
By the searing morning light.

Come What May

Interesting day
Art imitates life
Saw a play
Identified with the strife

Made a judgement call
Which seems to have paid off
Plans are now afoot
Water flows again through my trough

Who knows what will happen
When they finally come to fruition
I'll have to wait and see
'Tis my act of contrition

When the May Pole swings
I shall know the score
Until then I'll skip along
And think about it no more.

White Flag

Women are from Venus
Men are from Mars
Men have penises
Women wear bras

How these two creatures
Are to live in harmony
Is something which thus far
Has completely baffled me

It seems a constant struggle
To keep each other happy
One misunderstands the other
And then they both feel crappy

But when you are hetro
You yearn for the opposite sex
Yet when you find someone
It becomes so utterly complex

Can't live with them
Can't live without
Being in love's the best thing ever
Until there's something to row about

Then all hell breaks loose
Emotions flying high
Men run for the hills
Women start to cry

They think it's all over
And then perhaps it's not
First they break up
Then give it another shot

A merry-go-round
Of blood, sweat and tears
When to throw in the towel?
When to reconcile not disappear?

What's the magic formula?
To getting this crazy little thing right?
I'm tired of it all
I surrender, I won't fight.

The One

I don't believe I'll find 'the one'
For I believe he exists in me
The capacity to be alone
Is the way to set yourself free

Love is within you
Pure and abundant –
Tap into the force

And co-dependency
Will be redundant
And nothing will you have lost

Loving yourself will make you whole
Bringing you happiness
That doesn't hinge on someone else's whims
The form that is the best

Then should a 'special someone' come
You won't find it such a challenge
For they'll serve to complement you as oppose to 'complete' you
And you'll never lose your balance.

Fragile

Fragile flower being blown by the wind
To and fro, to and fro

Petals ruffling in the breeze –
Will they stay or will they go?

Slender stem swaying this way and that
Yet tightly gripped by the ground

Hold on tight – the storm can't last
The sun will soon come out

Droplets of rain cascade thick and fast
But it cleanses you as it flows

Into the earth to nourish your roots
So that you can continue to grow.

Calling Out

Calling out to the angels
To rain down tonight
Need a hand to hold
Before the morning light

Something is unfolding
I am helpless here
Need to find the strength
To live through what I fear

My faith is shaken
This world seems cruel
No explanation
So I'm reaching out to you

I'm calling out to the angels
To rain down on me
Lift me up when I can't stand
And I'm down on my knees

Calling out to the angels
To shine their guiding light
Lead the way out of this place
And spread their love tonight

Is this the time for prayer?
What I am praying for?
The strength to proceed
When I can do no more

The ticking of the clock
The minutes ebb away
Seconds pass but I'm paralysed
All I can do is wait

Am I mistaken?
Just a fool?
Feeling so jaded
So I'm reaching out to you

Calling out to the angels
To rain down on me
Lift me up when I can't stand
And I'm down on my knees

Calling out to the angels
If there is a God above
To hear my plea, rain down on me
Fill me with your love.

This Place

This place where you are going
I have never been
But I believe that you'll go on
In a different reality

I believe in the afterlife
And in angels and in heaven
I believe you'll find true love
I believe you will always be present

The spirit never dies
The soul is everlasting
The body is a skin
You simply will be shedding

And when you close your eyes
And finally go to sleep
You'll wake up in a dream
Where you will be at peace

Ecstasy will envelop you
You'll melt into such bliss
And rise above it all
And feel your father's kiss

And we're not far away
Just the other side of the door
You can visit any time
Even if we can't see you any more

Your daughters will know you are there
Because you'll live inside their hearts
And the memories they'll treasure
Will see them through the dark

You'll always be remembered
There's eternal life in that
You've made a tremendous impact
That simply is a fact

I love you to a million pieces
And wanted to say this to you
For I believe that something infinite
And profound is waiting for you.

Stephanie

My dearest friend
I love you so
I'm sorry that
You have to go

You've made a difference
To my life
You've cradled me
Through trouble and strife

You've bared your soul
And shared with me
Your deepest secrets
And hopefully found some peace

I'm honoured that
We found each other
My sister from
Another mother

My inspiration
And rock at times
Someone to laugh with
And someone to cry

Through the tears
And through the fun
I see your strength
How you don't run

Like a lioness
You face it all
Through your trials
You never fall

You keep it together
And do your best
When life is harsh
You pass the test

You hold on tight
And don't let go
The wonder of you
Is something I've never known.

Snapshot

Stephanie Pollard
With the Liza Minnelli eyes
The dazzling smile
So witty and so wise

The dancing queen
Who reigned supreme in Crouch End
A mother, daughter, sister
And to so many, a dear friend

An icon of style
A patron of the arts
An entrepreneur
A chef – so many parts

A chameleon
With widespread appeal
Who touched so many
For her spark was unreal

Hilarious and sweet
But the lioness could roar
Fiercely protective
Of those she adored

A no-nonsense woman
And bags of fun
We'll never forget her
She shone brighter than the sun.

Blowing In The Wind

Blowing in the wind
Flying in the breeze
Sailing on a cloud
Rustling through the trees

Free as a winged bird
Soaring through the sky
I'm sure you're there somewhere
Living formless as you fly

I felt your presence that night
That tingling on my skin
Those serene arms enfolding me
And I knew you were at peace within

I hear your name sometimes
Resounding in my head
And I know that you are close
And there's no need for the tears I shed

My dearest friend though I miss you
I know you're somewhere safe
And that we'll meet again
When it's my turn to visit that place.

Waves

The tide of grief
Like a wave comes and goes
Pulling at the heart strings
At times causing tears to flow

We can't predict when
This rain will fall
Anything could trigger the opening
Of the dam's walls

A passing memory
A fragrant scent
A similar face
Revisiting a place you both went

But the pain that we feel
When the showers come
Is born from the gift of having loved someone

And even though they've transitioned
To another plane
That love keeps us connected
Until we meet again

And that time will come
Of this I'm sure
When it's our turn to pass
Through that door

Until then may the angels
Lend you their wings

And cradle you from underneath
Forming a lifeboat that sings

To enable you to sail
Over the turbulent seas
And steer you on a course
To finding some peace.

Double Whammy

There's a hole in my life
Where he and she were
I miss them both much
Almost too much to bear

The two people with whom
I spent most of my time
My lover and my friend
One in heaven, one not mine

Unlike her
He will return
But to live without them both
Is a lesson I must learn

So twice I grieve
For my two special peeps
As my life they both leave
Whom I loved beyond heaps

Well, I'll cherish the memories
Of the good times we shared
Those spent with him
Those spent with her

Those spent together –
The best times of all
He brought us together –
What a fortuitous call

Thus I thank him so much
For giving me that gift
She enhanced my life hugely
And I am grateful for this.

Sitting Ducks

Oh, fuck a duck
I love that bloody expression
For all of us are sitting like one
Though we do a good impression

Of being in control
Keeping calm and carrying on
When the reality of it is
A bullet could at any time come

And knock us off our perch
Scattering feathers everywhere
Upsetting the apple cart
Having us tearing out our hair

If we're lucky enough, that is
To survive the initial blast
It's like playing Russian Roulette
Every day could be our last

So party like it's the end of the world
Love that boy, love that girl
Sod that job if it's making you blue
Eat that cake, have those shoes

Take that holiday
Buy that car
Live it up
Act like a star

For all of us are A-listers
Action heroes dodging bullets
Life is a flaming mine field
So grab it by the gullet

Use your time wisely
It's limited after all
Make every second count
For even the great ones fall.

Travelling

Somehow we made it through
And reached our respective destinations
Separated, it's true
But intact in our new locations

And I, for one, feel enriched
By that part of our journey we shared
The pleasure was worth the pain
I have no desire to be spared

We needed each other
For whatever the reason
Enjoyed a haitus
A hay-making season

But all life is transient
It ebbs and it flows
Seasonal cycles
Will come and then go

Relationships
Will blossom and fade
Sure as the night
Will follow the day

I am just happy
That by pure chance
We met along the way
And enjoyed a wonderful dance

And I say this to all
My compadres in life
The good, the bad, the ugly
The trouble and the strife

Thank you for the colours
You wove into my fabric
Thank you for the legends
Who've helped me walk this labyrinth

And thanks in anticipation
For all that is yet to come
I'm ready to embrace you
A new chapter has begun.

View From The Plateau

Questioning who I am
What it's all about
Living in the here and now
Trying to figure it out

Feeling pain but also love
Seeing the beauty in life
Witnessing things I can only contemplate
The struggles, the worry and strife

Change is in the air
But I've reached a firm plateau
And here I'll stay until such time
I feel the urge to go.

The Present

When you have no power
And things are beyond your control
All you can do is nothing
You just have to let go

The present is yours
And it is a gift
All you have is now

Try to be in the moment
Try to live there somehow

You may not find it easy
It can be hard at times
But doing it might help
To give you peace of mind

Try to forget the future
Try to forget the past
For we have no way of knowing
How long the present will last.

2016

It's cold outside
And I'm chilled to the bone
Christmas is a-coming
Oh, how this year has flown

But 2016
You've been something of a bitch
Taking all the good ones
It's been something of a blitz

Then we had Brexit
Followed by Trump
You couldn't make it up
Perhaps we all should jump

Well, it can't get any worse
There's only a month of you left
And I'm going to make it count
And do my level best

To end you on a high
And send you off in style
Although you don't deserve it
Cause, frankly, you were vile

But I'll celebrate anyway
For nothing lasts forever
Even the bad times end
And if we're wise, they'll bring us together.

Cruel Yule

Where did it all go wrong?
Christmas more macabre than Halloween
It's become a commercial nightmare
Instead of a nativity scene

A tacky, money spinning business
Bedecked with flashing neon lights
Like a bad day out gambling in Blackpool
Instead of a time to put the world to rights

In retail it starts in July
When they open the Christmas shop
Flogging the tinsel and spinning the tunes
Oh, please, someone make it stop!

And now, in November, some erect the tree
Not twelve days before like it used to be
The magic of Christmas eroded away
What would baby Jesus, Mary and Joseph say?

What happened to simple carols
And dining on festive fare?
Curling up with loved ones
All cosy and warm somewhere?

Counting all our blessings
Learning lessons, feeling thankful?
Not wearing out our feet
Pacing malls in a mad scramble

Of frenzied unbridled spending
Like possessed demonic trolls
Bingeing and consuming
Black Friday, January sales

No time for rest at all
Or spiritual contemplation
No time for togetherness
Just indulgence and inflation

Of prices and of waistlines
Whilst souls are starved of nutrition
The true meaning dead and buried
The decay of the human condition

It's grating on me already
And December has barely begun
Hence why I'm slinging my hook
And spending it an Ashram.

22/03

Weird 24 hours
Pendulum-like emotions
Westminster attack
A warped display of 'devotion'

Londoners carry on
Shaken but not stirred
Hearts go out to the victims
And the heroes who've now been heard

It ain't the first time
We've been hit
Certainly won't be the last

But we'll stand tall
Rise above this
Then file it away in the past

Onwards and upwards
For troupers we are
We choose to live here
We'll deal with the scars

You can't keep us down
We mean to live free
And that's what we'll do
Everybody!

We'll go about our business
The same as before
We won't live in fear
Or cower behind locked doors

I remember 7/7
Like it was yesterday
I still take the tube
Come what may

You didn't beat us then
You certainly won't now
You're in a minority
You can't take us down.

Wired But No Sound

Watching Eurovision
But the tv's broken down
Got a lovely picture
But got no bloody sound

Maybe that's a good thing
At least my ears won't bleed
At least I will be spared
From 50% of the cheese

Lots of flags and tinsel
Patriotism abounds
Everyone is buzzing
Still got no bloody sound

Special effects
Dazzle on the stage
Happy, smiling people
But all I feel is rage

Still got no bloody sound
So singing to myself
Trying to lip read
And work the lyrics out

Tinkering with wires
Trying to fix this issue
But I'm no techno whiz
I could totally rip a tissue

Missing all the quips
By cheeky Graham Norton
Kind of kills the mood
My little fuse is shortened

Could just go to bed
But wired to the moon
My triple macchiato at 6
Was a really stupid move

Wtf – a gorilla?
But where's the big drum kit?
I want to hear In The Air Tonight
If he's wearing that, the twit

That said I've got no sound
So even if it played
I wouldn't be able to hear it
I'm seriously dismayed.

Reflections

The present currently a mirror
Reflecting shades of myself back at me

The light of my mind a flicker with insight
Illumination highlighting the different aspects of my soul
laid bare for all to see

The moonlight glistening on the water
Rippling pictures fade in and out
A movie of notions and thoughts playing out from within
the depths of my psyche

Obliterating past patterns of behaviour hopefully to be re-
placed in the future with a more conscious wave of being

The shedding of a skin
The raw exposure of a new layer acclimatising to this new
found perception

Healing afoot yet still fragile and shaken from the initial
impact of the light piercing and shattering the glacial pyr-
amid I was incased in

Dangling from the silver thread of a spider's web swinging through space and time surrounded by sparkling stars

Suspended for now enjoying the spectacular view across the horizon

Happiness.

The Now

Energy flows
Where attention goes
The mind like a laser
Beaming out those
Thoughts into the atmosphere
Until they manifest
Whatever their vibration
Dictates what you get

Like invites like
The law of attraction
Plain and simple
A chemical reaction
If you want something good
To come your way
Condition your thoughts
Positive things to say

Be an observer
Listen to the chat
Inside your head
Call the negative back

Cancel it out
Before it's in the post
Send out something beautiful
That you desire most

And it will come back
Tenfold to you
Imbuing your world
With a magical hue
Live in the Now
Forget about the past
Don't stress the future
It may not come to pass

All that we have
Is THIS moment in time
Own it, live it
And tranquility you'll find.

Escape

A brand new day is born
The sun has now arisen
Who knows what's to come
In this perception prism

Light refracted this way and that
People intermingling through it
Riffing off each other as they go
Their inner worlds reacting to it

Nature the observer to it all
Quietly poised in the ground
Tranquil and noble it stands tall
And doesn't make a sound

The bustling city alive with noise
Money to be made
How I yearn to leave it all behind
And return to my sacred place.

Avalon

Avalon was calling
Beckoning me there
Thus I obeyed the summons
And visited somewhere

I thought I knew nothing of
Yet had an urge right now to see
I knew not why at the time
But once there it seemed meant to be

It all made perfect sense
A feeling of belonging
Something for which I'd been searching
A yearning and a longing

Magical things occurred
Like the angelic rhapsody
Resounding from the tor
How could it possibly be?

And filled through the crown was I
By a fluid warm and pure
Weighted to the ground
By the force at which it poured

An energy then cursed through me
Reverberating inside
Charged did I become
My soul alight, on fire

Why? What does it mean?
Was it imagined or was it real?
You may find it hard to believe
Indeed it was surreal

But one thing is for sure
I'll make the pilgrimage again
When the time is right
When that message is sent

Back to my spiritual home
Where my heart and soul can be nourished
To be with the kin I encountered
To be nurtured and encouraged.

Good Vibrations

Lost in music
In a trance
Feeling the vibes
The freedom of dance

Shaking it out
Going wild
Riding the wave
Kundalini fired

Eyes wide shut
Turning within
Expressing the animal
The moment in

Feeling the beat
Stamping it out
Letting go
In no doubt

That in this place
On the floor
Is all you need
Nothing more.

Hope

When hope springs
Grab it with both hands
It will guide you forward
Help you realise your plans

It puts a skip in your step
Gives you motivation
It's a driving force
Helping you reach your destination

When hope is lost
Find some more
If one closes
Open another door

Go with your gut
Listen to your intuition
Observe the signs
In your peripheral vision

Never lose hope
It's a bottomless well
Just look for the source
Find the swell

Hope is all you need
To help you get by
It's like a little beacon
Lighting up the sky!

Gratitude

Looking through the window
I see the crescent moon
Peering at me from behind a rooftop
Housing someone else's room

Pure and white, a blinding light
Shining in the sky
Pulling upon my psyche
As I contemplate my life

The other day it was full
Super and complete
Now it appears to be waning
As I prepare for sleep

I'm noticing its cycle
For the first time in a while
And thinking about what it symbolises
And inwardly I smile

The sunset also drew me in
Its beauty was so fine
I'm thankful for the little things
That make this journey sublime.

The Elements

Be like water
Go with the flow
Where the river takes you
You cannot possibly know

Be like the breeze…
Light as air
Ride that wave
Without a care

Live for the day
You may not see tomorrow
No point dwelling
On the pain and sorrow

Take it as it comes
A blessing in disguise
Find that silver lining
You won't believe you eyes

Fire purifies
Lightening breaks the shackles
A Phoenix will often rise
From the ashes of the battle

And if you are still standing
When all has come to pass
Thank you're lucky stars
You weren't obliterated by the blast

Then start over again
You got a second chance
Grab it by the horns
And bloody learn to dance!

Destination Bliss

I feel I've got my mojo back
Maybe found a calling
A new found sense of direction
On track at last not falling

Into the bleak abyss
Where life just has no meaning
I'm moving forward not stagnating
I've found something to believe in

A driving force
To who knows where
Destination irrelevant

It's about the journey
The getting there
In case you missed my point

What a delight to reignite that spark
That was lost along the way
To regain that spring inside your step
And bounce from day to day

To rediscover that zest for life
That escaped you for a while
And find something to smile about
To see you through your trials

How good it feels right now
To breath and be alive
If I could bottle it I would sell it
So you could join me on this ride

Sharing is caring after all
And this is such a very good feeling
I hope that by expressing it
It'll rub off on you, get you dreaming

For surely we all need dreams
And at times the courage to pursue them
We don't want the knocks to snuff them out
Even if we never achieve them

Ascertain what you love to do
It'll get your energy flowing
Find your passion and go with it
If you want to reap, keep sowing

Follow your bliss
And surely you'll thrive
What better a way live

For life is for living
Isn't it?
So do it and not a f**k give.

Blessed Lunacy

Experiencing divine madness
My mind again is blown
Wide awake, sudden knowing
Intuition heightened, aglow

Employing words the catalyst
I've been playing them you see
Words are magical instruments
They unlock, they are a key

Composing music
Creating rhymes
Making some noise
The volume up high

Interpreting and decoding
Symbolism and signs
A flash of illumination
The veil thinner, no longer blind

Feeling charged, plugged in
To a higher power
The moon card now at play
Bewitched am I this hour

Colliding with a soulmate
Activated something inside
Catapulted me skywards
I got so freakin high

Heavenly was the experience
I've yet to come back down
I'm out of my body it seems
I left it there on the ground

I burst into song
Sing from my soul
Unable to stop
I have no control

Such good vibrations all around
I lap them up, feel alive
Whatever I'm on its natural
No need for cacao this time

Reconnected have I with my source
My heart chakra beats like a drum
Vibrations are raised, I'm lifted up
I've craved some of this for so long

We can't always get we want
But we might find we get what we need
There's a silver lining in every cloud
Blessings come in disguise, literally.

Words

Words are incantations, catalysts
Loaded guns
Their power is boundless
Second to none

They set forces in motion
Start and stop wars
They are evocative
Emotive, impactful and more

What you're trying to convey
May be misconstrued
Units of language are they
Often misunderstood

Lost in translation
Can they sometimes get
When discharged they are potent
With the potential to be ill met

Use them we must
If we want to communicate
But select them with care
Before allowing them to escape

Once released into the ether
All control is lost
What you intended to convey
May get star-crossed

So speak from the heart
Write from a place of love
Then you can be sure
Their impact will be good.

Contact

The channel is open
I read you loud and clear
Transmission received
We're back on air

Wireless communication
Got you on the phone
Finally found your number
ET phoned home

Radiohead
Got it tuned in
To your frequency now
I can hear you again

Back online
Able to download
The files that you sent
That were written in code

Managed to unencrypt it
Opened up the safe
Found the secret password
To unlock the star-gate

Access granted
It would seem
To a library of knowledge
Or is this all just a dream?

Seeing Stars

Stars are alive
Emitting light
Emanating messages
As they sparkle in the night

Beacons in the dark
Illuminating the earth
Imparting wisdom and knowledge
Listen, interpret, learn

Set the dial on your radio
Turn on, tune in, drop out
Logon on to the cosmos
It's easy when you know how

Open up the floodgates
Allow it to flow in
Embrace it with your heart
You'll never be the same again

Free your mind to the possibilities
That the intangible does exist
Believe in the incomprehensible
Experience the bliss.

Twisting The Melon

Subliminal, sublime
Toying with hidden meaning
Making up for lost time
Too long have I been sleeping

Once awakened from a slumber
You cannot help but see
Things as they really are –
But what is reality?

Isn't it subjective?
Dependent upon your perception?
Mirrors are everywhere
Reflecting light from every direction

Some are blinded by the sight
Shrink from it back into the dark
They fear it like it is their kryptonite
If only they could open their hearts…

The Others reach out to embrace it
And bask there in its presence
At opposite ends of the spectrum
Yet interconnected, correlessence

If you can see what I see
Hear the message I'm giving
Perhaps it will set you free
From any unease in which you are living

Try it, open up your mind
Experience is there for the taking
I'm offering you a ride
Of you it could be the making.

Hello?

Send me the instrumental
And I'll write you a lyric
Let's do a collaboration
Of mind and spirit

I want to make people dance
Move them in some way
Get them up on their feet
Jumping around, at play

Sending out this call
To the universe
Setting out my intention
In the hope I'll be heard

Let's join hands
Create something epic
This is my dream –
It could be yours too if you let it!

The Holiday

Been away with the fairies
Had my head in the clouds
On a dream trip
Didn't want to come back down

Took a vacation
To another plane
Felt so good to explore
The inner realms of the brain

Nothing like getting away from it all
Nothing like running free
Trying to solve life's mysteries
Imaginings, fantasies

On the wings of a unicorn
I flew into outer space
Let me tell you this –
It is a wonderful place.

'Jest'

Many a true word
Is said in jest
Deny it, you may
But too much you protest

Don't think me incapable
Of ascertaining your true intention
I can feel the vibration
Of what you failed to mention

Transmuted did it to me
The true meaning of your words
The humour you tried to conceal it with
Fell on 'deaf' ears

Just letting you know
That I received the 'real' message
Make of that what you will
Just don't forget it.

Rattled

Like acid rain the venom dripped
From the rattled snake's tongue
A deadly poison, no antidote
The damage had been done

He was provoked, felt threatened
Lashed out in self defence
Survival instinct activated
Too late for recompense

He felled his assailant with one bite
Sinking in his fangs
A lethal injection of dynamite
His 'victim' could not withstand

The reptile, spent, then slithered away
Without a backward glance
To lick his wounds in safety
Leaving nothing more to chance

Did he feel remorse?
Is he sentient?
It was an act of natural law
Which, perhaps he could not prevent.

Message In A Bottle

I sent out a warning
A cautionary note
To handle me with care
Or away would I float

That's all it was
Nothing more, nothing less
It wasn't a threat
Just a point I wished to impress

Upon his subconscious mind
To convey I was in the loop
That neither the wool pull over my eyes
Nor me could he dupe

And there shall it be left
Nothing more to say
What happens now
Is for fate to outplay.

Sayonara

Frenemy, frenemy there you are
Your true colours finally shown
An ugly palate of murky shades
I'd suspected but not fully known

Your guard let down
They came to light
In an outpouring of harboured rage

That clearly had
Been festering inside
Until this putrid and vile display

Like a rocket gone off
And a man possessed
You listed all of my 'sins'

Instructed me
To live vacuously
Or be cast out with the bins

I chose the latter
For not for me
Are 'friends' of the fair weather kind

A friend should be someone
Who's got your back
You can laugh with and unwind

But more than that
They must show respect
Even when times get tough

Never must
That line be crossed
Or the whole thing will combust

And combust it did
In spectacular style
Past the point of no return

As one by one
Insult by insult
Every bridge did you burn

Thus cut loose are you
And banished for life
No regrets and no great loss

In separating
The wheat from the chaff
New horizons can I cross

Out with the old
And in with the new
As the energy starts to shift

Already they come
The influx begins
Of new friends bearing their gifts

So sayonara
And good luck too
As we walk our separate paths

I shed you now
For pastures new
Never to look back.

Thoughts

Here's a thought –
You can keep your penny
This one's for free
Like you, I have many

I'm giving it away
'Cause you know what thought did?
It played a little tune
On your radiohead

The volume was high
I was locked to your station
Thoughts are alive
Full of vibrations

I heard it loud and clear
You didn't need to shout
Reverberating through my ears
Calling you out

Exposing your true feelings –
What a revelation
I guess telepathy is real –
Something of a complication

So bear that in mind
Next time you put me down
Thoughts have wings
Of this I'm in no doubt.

Weirdos

Weird and wonderful
Off the wall
Round peg
In a square hole

What to do
When you don't fit in
Throw in the towel?
Start again?

Or stick it out
Develop a thick skin
Grin and bear it
Take it on the chin?

There's always one
Who spoils the fun
Veiled barbed comments
But the damage is done

A wolf in sheep's clothing
Or rather a suit
Calls it 'banter'
When putting in the boot

Seeks an audience
Braver after a beer
Can't deal with alternatives
Finds them 'queer'

His problem not mine
My motto is this:
Deal with it, dude
Live and let live.

Dirty Cash

The root of all evil
The haves, the have nots
The issue of money
Ties people in knots

Friends go to war
Enemies stay so
The politics of dosh
Are a snake pit of dough

Which nestles underneath
A veneer of calm
Hissing and spitting
Fangs engaged to do harm

Careful you don't fall in
To the deadly trap
Keep it shut
Be sure to do that

Or at your peril
You'll slide into hell
The reptiles will coil around you
And crush you where you fell

Punctured, suffocated
Bones all smashed
Poisoned with venom
Pulped til you gasp

The distribution of wealth
Never did sit right
But them's the rules
We can fight all we like

I didn't make them up
I'm just playing the game
Doing what's needed
To survive, I've no shame

Ain't begging nor stealing
Nobody died
You do what you must
When engaged on this ride

If I had my way
We'd all have the same
Work if we wanted to
Instead of being pimped, in chains

Slaves to a system
Intrinsically flawed
Put in place
By privileged overlords

Totally out of touch
Or who don't give a f**k
About the average Jo
Who is down on their luck

Trying to make ends meet
In an increasingly costly world
Where the posts keep moving
Until you can't score a goal

You may say I'm a dreamer
Well I'm not the only one
I can dream all I want
Because dreams spur you on.

The Positive

Crushing disappointment
When people let you down
At the eleventh hour
And no one else is around

What else can you do but sit with it
And try not to take it to heart
Turn your mind to something else
Channel it into art

Accentuate the positive
Eliminate the negative
Find something good and go with it
Try not to fall apart

Everyone has their issues in life
Circumstances change, troubles and strife
Keep in your centre, don't deviate
Fingers crossed things will turn out great!

Friendlies

Lazy weekend
Chatting to chums
Near and far
Sitting on my bum

Now off to a show
To meet another
And chin-wag some more
About life and lovers

It's good to catch up
And reconnect
Doesn't have to be everyday
But we never forget

The ties that bind us
Even though we've moved on
Lives in different places
But friendship still strong

Love them all
Wherever they are
Plans to meet again
Whether by ferry, train or car

Or just popping round the corner
To have a little drink
It's good to have chums
Scattered around methinks

So thank you to all
I'm blessed to know
Love y'all to bits
You keep my wee heart aglow!

The Fool

The ripple effect expanded
Across the surface of the lake
Something had make an impact
Left an impression in its wake

I knew not what the cause
Simply observed the movement did I
In reflective mode as I sat
By the water, my thoughts passing by

Calming was its motion
Soothing to my mind
And there in that little spot
A sense of tranquillity did I find

I allowed this sensation to wash over me
And felt my fervour cool
Whilst I drew a card from my deck
And saw that it was the Fool.

My Addicition

Thinking about my addiction
And how to kick the habit
How to stop consuming it
Before I'm totally ravaged

It's making me sick I'm aware of that
But now I cannot break it
I'm reliably told it takes willpower
But I just can't seem to make it

I'm aware of all its triggers
And I want to stop this action
But doing it just sometimes
Gives me satisfaction

Now I'm making excuses
When I've only myself to blame
I lit the stick, sucked on it
Now I must face the pain

The buzz isn't always nice
Sometimes it just feels toxic
But I'll still scavenge to get some
Whilst I wonder if I've lost it

I've tried reading books and bought a vape
But thus far I have failed
So still those drags I will take
Even though I have travailed

It makes me feel shitty
It makes me feel crap
It's so absurd
I could almost laugh

It's out of control
It's getting obscene
I need some help
To quit nicotine.

Tech No!

The age of technology
Is a pile of s**t

It's so messed up
It makes you spit

All it does
Is make you more busy

The flow of information's
So fast you go dizzy

Wired to machines
From dawn til dark

Phones stuck to ears
Fingers constantly parked

On touch-screens, keyboards
Buttons - no rest

Constantly plugged in
The more we become obsessed

Does it make us faster
More competent?

No, it makes us angry,
Too available – we resent

The relentless interruptions
Whatever time of day

Leisure time consumed
In an insatiable way

A billion tons of admin is
All it generates

Do everything yesterday
It's always too late

Red tape piles up
Inevitably breaks the chain

Too much to think about
We all feel the strain

Is this why we came here
To be enslaved?

If time doesn't exist
Why isn't enough saved?

For rest, contemplation
– the space to just be

Without some jumped up tosser
Making more demands on we?

Too many hours
Of too many days

Entangled by petty bureaucracy
Correcting errors that were made

Because nobody gives a damn
About their jobs anymore

Too exhausted, disillusioned
From being someone else's whore

Too many people
Bleeding services dry

Too many mouths forced
By deprivation to cry

Too many souls disconnected
From the light

Who can save us now
From this hellish plight?

We've created a world
That thrives on greed

The crop already consumed
When barely out of seed

Everywhere someone screaming
Out their desperate need

Like locusts we rape
And pillage in order to feed

It can't go on forever
Something's got to give

I despair of this world
In which we currently live

One day the whole thing
Will simply implode

Dragging all of us down
Into a black hole

Is there light
At the end of this tunnel?

Will salvation somehow find
A fitting channel?

You're asking the wrong one
– I'm merely stating a fact

Where is this fabled saviour,
If one exists, to remedy that?

Hangry

Fook me, I'm so ravenous
I actually could die
Hangry am I as hell
In desperate need of pie

Craving me some stodge
And all things well unhealthy
Man-food's calling out my name
Stand back or Please, God help me!

Contemplating Chinese
Or maybe fish n chips
Got to be mahoosive
And greasy and delish

Special Fried Rice perhaps
With chips and curry sauce
Harking back to my childhood
We loved it then, of course

Might seem a little odd
Now I've defected south
But back then in The Boro
It brought water to the mouth

Actually, a Parmo
Right now would be amazing
With chips and garlic sauce –
Christ, I'm salivating!

Chips becoming a theme
Reoccurring at this time
Chips with everything
Or just chips would actually be fine

Cause I'm famished now, you see
And it's driving me bloody nuts
So off the bus I go
In search of all the goods

I'll see you a little bit later
When I'm feeling satisfied
Having binged me on some junk
And all things lush and fried.

Toothgate

Been to the dentist
For a Re: root canal
Had needles in my gums
To numb me out
He's been digging and a-drilling
Into my molar
I really cannot wait
For this saga to be over!

When he Re-packed the tooth
I was in pain
Had to go back
To have it drained
That didn't work
And now it's infected
Not gonna deny I'm
Feeling dejected

Agony ensued
Three sleepless nights
Been back four times
To get it put right

He opened up the tooth
Again and again
But that's not workin –
I'm still in pain

Antibiotics
Drugs aplenty
I'm going up the wall
A little demented
When will the story end?
Can't take anymore
Feeling so rancid
I'm on the floor

Gotta go back Tuesday
To finish the job
Costing me a fortune
Think I have been robbed!

Stumped

Done my back in
Hurts like hell
So soon after Toothgate
I'm miserabelle

Don't know how it happened
But it sure did
Can't bend down
Without looking like a flid

Hobbling around
Is so unattractive
Cannee go to the gym
Condemned to being inactive

Gonna get flabby
If I ain't careful
Gotta stop munching
Feeling annoyed, obese and awful

Can't wear heels
Without feeling pain
Contemplating getting
A flamin zimmerframe

Must be getting old
Could be osteoporosis
Add it to the list
Of ailments I'm diagnosed with

Alexander Technique
Is sounding a good option
Have my spine stretched out
And maybe put in traction

How long this will last?
I have no bloody clue
But I sure can't swing from the chandeliers –
I can barely go to the loo

I need an MOT,
A service, an overhaul
Gonna book myself into Kwik Fit
Let them tinker with it all

That should do the trick
They sorted out my car
It's running like a dream
Now it's my turn, thank you, Ta!

Maybe it was all that dancing
Wot done it, hmmm, perhaps –
The field was so uneven
And I wasn't wearing flats!

That'll learn me, I suppose
Next time I'll know better
But boogying's good for the soul
And us midgets feel the pressure

Of not being able to see
Through the person in front's head
And having to endure
Having stumps instead of legs

So platforms are a must
Whatever the conditions
We suffer for our lack of height
And wear them on every expedition

When I say 'we' I mean I
And not in the royal sense
But let's not get me started on wee
For I just might cause offence.

Birds In a Gilded Cage

Trying to make sense of it all
And how I fit into the puzzle
If life is a tapestry
With whom is the weaver I struggle

For the world seems but a web at times
In which us mortals are caught
With spiders presiding above us
Oppressive overlords

Conflicts and wars
Pepper society
When all the majority desire
Is peace, love and harmony

But the prominent pacifists die:
Lennon, Jackson, Marley...
Those that are left behind
Bereft find it hard to keep trying

To bring about the change
Overdue, still out of reach
The majority are discontent
Disillusioned at this defeat

When the balance will shift
I simply do not know
But something has got to give:
We reap what we sow.

Wandering Hands in La La Land

Wandering hands
Preying pervs
Surely now in La La Land
More will be unearthed

It's about time this rot
Was wheedled out
It shouldn't be what the profession
Is all about

The casting couch needs
To become obsolete
Shagging your way to the top
Never sat well with me

'Tis a plague on the profession
Afflicting women all too much
Why should we endure
Someone chancing a touch?

Groping you under the guise
It'll get you more work –
Don't these men realise
They are clearly sick jerks?

Abusing their power
And position in this way
Intimidating their victims
Into subjugation for pay

Thank God for Equity
If you have the balls to fight
I didn't once upon a time
But that doesn't make it right

Women must unite
And find their voice
Speak up and speak out –
You have a choice!

Displaced

'Living' on the gum-stained streets
Invisible to passing crowds
A lone, malnourished, child-woman sleeps
Why is this injustice allowed?

Eyes rolled back in her head
A jaundiced pallor presides on her cheeks
The grim reaper is surely close by
Lying in wait for this girl is so weak

Striding by in their hoards
Commuters, oblivious, it seems
To the plight of the smacked-out girl
Having hallucinogenic dreams

Her filthy, rain sodden mattress
Is inadequate to say the least
Though sickened to my very stomach
I walk on like the rest of the sheep

This image ingrained in my brain
Incessantly preys on my mind
Going home I check she's 'ok'
That's a laugh, she's so clearly not fine

I worry for her every night
That she'll expire before the morning dew
So intoxicated at times it's a fright
But what can I alone possibly do?

This wretch is the tip of the iceberg
Many more bed down there all the time
Makeshift homes under the railway bridge
Amongst the pigeons and rats and the grime

They furnish their plots with cuddly toys
Trinkets that belong in a house
Their food stowed beside them,
Carefully placed
So as not to be stolen by a mouse

Some mornings some sport a fresh wound
A black eye, swollen ankle and the like
Sitting ducks to be targeted by youths
Tanked up, in the mood for a fight

"Not my problem! I'm alright Jack!
Certainly in anger should we not look back!"

But surely it is yet we turn a blind eye?
So another one succumbs, is consumed and then dies

"It's not alright, Jack! It's a f**king disgrace!
In so rich a society to be so desperately displaced!"

So many of us live on the edge
A pay cheque or two away:

"Get a grip, deal with it, Jack!
Even now it's already too late".

Red Sky

A Sahara/strawberry sky
Hangs over London Town
Shrouded in a sultry fog
As from my tower I peer out

The view across the city
Takes on a Blade Runneresque hue
As fiction threatens to come to life
With Ophelia passing through

The mood reactively ominous
The calm before the storm
Nobody wishes anyone
To come to any harm

The street lights all aglow
Though it's only 4pm
Eerily silent and unseasonably warm
Are we facing Armageddon?

Red layers of ancient sand
Sail in on the balmy wind
From the deserts of Africa
Of biblical times do they remind

Thus this hurricane adopts a fleece
So innocuous does she seem
As did her namesake in death
When floating down the stream

But like the flowers she loved so
This beauty we cannot trust
For it has the power to maim and kill
When its eye is at last upon us.

Being Spritely

'What planet is he from?'
Some might say
'Talking all that chat
Behaving in that that way!

He must be out of his mind
Nuts, barking mad
The filth he comes out with
The cheek of the lad!

He's really lost it now
Should go back to telling jokes
Credibility
Puff! Up In smoke'

Hmmm, do I think
Perhaps he has a point
Maybe he is 'touched'
By that which anoints

There's method in madness
Many a true word said in jest
And he's the most famous of them all
With his hair such a mess

I too am a Pixie
And ponder this do I –
What planet is he from?
The same one as mine.

Branded

Russell Brand
You make me quiver
My heart beats fast
I shake and shiver

Ever since
I saw your face
In 2006
I've been displaced

From Big Brother's Big Mouth
To You've Got Issues
To Brighton and Back
And London – all venues

I follow your story
Everywhere
For some strange reason
I really do care

Your spiritual journey
Political battles
Your ups and downs
You're prances and prattles

You tickle me pink
You're a dream to behold
A groupie I've become
I love you tenfold

And though you're a dad
And your heart is now taken
You will never ever
By me be forsaken

My 'evil' twin
And idol to boot
I watch you from afar
And I salute

The man that you are
So perfect yet flawed
Prone to mishaps
That are never ignored

So similar to me
In so many ways
You never fail to bring
A huge smile to my face.

Earth Angel

He was beamed into my living room
And bewitched me then and there
Overcome with butterflies
All I could do was stare

Never had I beheld such beauty
In so masculine a man
I couldn't take my eyes off him
And was beyond overcome

I vowed then I would find him
And meet him in the flesh
Like he'd cast a spell on me
I was in him enmeshed

He seemed to possess my mind
Infiltrated all my thoughts
Every minute of every day
With the urge to meet him I fought

Then lo and behold opportunity knocked
And I acquired tickets to his show
Wild horses could never have stopped me
I knew I had to go

Dressed to impress off I went
A sense of purpose in my step
I knew not why I felt such a pull
Towards a man I'd never met

But in the studio it all became clear
As I trembled in my seat
The stage was empty yet my pulse raced
My heart pounded with every beat

Suddenly I felt his aura
Sweep across the room
With such a force it knocked me sideways
And a vision into my mind zoomed

Of a magnificent dark angel
With huge opalescent wings
Spanning the width of the earth
Purple, black, iridescent green

Almost like a peacock
It's feathers refracted the light
I felt such tremendous power
No star ever shone so bright

And then the man himself
Appeared at the top of the stairs
And made his entrance majestically
As he descended to the earth

Some liken him to Jesus
And he admits to the Messiah Complex
Lord knows if prophecies come true
This earth angel could he be resurrect

That said I'm prone to fantasise
And fevers of the brain
This could be but a dream
Though it happened all the same.

Rents

"They f**k you up
Your mam and dad"
According to the poem / book

Where the stalk
deposits you
Is random and pot luck

'You cannot choose your family'
But some believe you do
Before you incarnate this life –
This may or may not be true

I know I've toiled with mine
But oft they've been my heroes
I've loved and loathed them at the same time
Awarding them tens or zeros

I've abandoned ship
Then crawled back in a heap
They've built me up
And made me weak

I've sometimes misunderstood
Or the roles have been reversed
I've been their referee at times
And seen them at their worst

They can drive me to distraction
But I know that they are there
I know I'm lucky to have them both
God help me when they're elsewhere

Not being a parent myself
I can't possibly relate
To the mantle they undertook
When they chose to procreate

But that they did
And here I am
A product of their union

We're in this together
'Til death do us part
Blood our substance of this fusion

And indebted to them am I
The only constant I've ever known
They've made me who I am
Respect here must be shown.

'God'

Like the God of the Old Testament
Prone can you be to wrath
You're temperament unpredictable
Too infrequently do you laugh

But in my very creation
Did you have a hand
Thus I will always be thankful
Even if I don't understand

Why you are like you are
They broke the mold with you
A force of nature so powerful
At times some damage can you do

Indeed you too are a diamond
Unique, but in your case raw
Alas, you need refinement
But your beauty do I also adore

Still a work in progress
To polish you with love I have tried
But your edges, sharp, can cut deep
Even when wax is applied

Protective gloves I must wear
The closer I come to you
Handle you with care
Though precious, when sparkling you do

Have the ability to burn
For your element is combustive
Like a firework are you
Full of gunpowder, oft mistrusted

So forgive me if I am wary
I realise that you mean well
I love you even when you are scary
Know you wear a protective shell

Prickly on the outside
To protect the softness you fiercely guard
A bulldog you keep at your gate
I know not why you find it so hard
To express your true emotions
But ultimately you do
And live with that I must
For we're family, thick and thin through

So I worship you from afar
For at times you drive me mad
But I'm also grateful to have you –
My one and only Dad.

My Gem

How do I encapsulate
Just what you mean to me?
There are no words in existence
Quite worthy enough for thee

For you are as the sun
The giver of my life
Your radiance sublime
My anchor in times of strife

You love me unconditionally
Your warmth always filters through
Even when clouds obscure your face
You're dazzling innate smile radiates too

I love you with all of my heart
I thank you from its base
For everything you've ever done for me
For your beauty and your grace

A class act you truly are
A rare diamond here uncovered
So blessed am I to call you mine,
'Best friend', 'sister', Mother.

The End.

About The Author

Rachel Rhodes-Puckett is a lyricist, writer, professional actress, singer, spiritualist and self-proclaimed professional bimbette! ;)

Printed in Poland
by Amazon Fulfillment
Poland Sp. z o.o., Wrocław

50390080R00106